THE FACTS ABOUT

ADOPTION

BY
Gail B. Stewart

EDITED BY
Anita Larsen

CONSULTANT
Elaine Wynne, M.A., Licensed Psychologist

CRESTWOOD HOUSE
New York

CIP
LIBRARY OF CONGRESS CATALOGING IN PUBLICATION DATA

Stewart, Gail
  Adoption

  (The facts about)
  Includes index.
  SUMMARY: Discusses the processes by which people can adopt, who adopts, sources for adoptive children, and other aspects of adoption as seen from both children's and parents' sides.
  1. Adoption — United States — Juvenile literature. [1. Adoption.] I. Title. II. Series.
HV875.55.S74   1989   362.7'34'0973—dc20   89-1525
ISBN 0-89686-443-X

PHOTO CREDITS

Cover: Third Coast Stock Source: Scott Witte
The Image Works: (Bob Daemmrich) 4, 9, 24, 37; (Lorraine Rorke) 16; (Patsy Davidson) 44
Third Coast Stock Source: (Lens Photo) 10; (Thomas Lemke) 20, 43; (Scott Witte) 27; (Kent DuFault) 31
DRK Photo: (D. Cavagnaro) 15
FPG International: 32

Copyright © 1989 by Crestwood House, Macmillan Publishing Company

All rights reserved. No part of this book may be reproduced or transmitted in any form or by any means, electronic or mechanical, including photocopying, recording, or by any information storage and retrieval system, without permission in writing from the Publisher.

CRESTWOOD HOUSE

Macmillan Publishing Company
866 Third Avenue
New York, NY 10022
Collier Macmillan Canada, Inc.

Produced by Carnival Enterprises
Printed in the United States of America
First Edition
10 9 8 7 6 5 4 3 2 1

TABLE OF CONTENTS

Beginnings 5
Adoption — Nothing New 10
Apprentices 11
Poorhouses: The Shame of the Cities 12
The Orphanage and Beyond 13
Who Adopts? 15
Deciding to Adopt 17
Where Are the Babies? 19
On the List 21
The Birth Mother 23
Don't Decide Now 25
A Gift of Life 26
How Does It Feel? 28
Wondering 30
Words Can Sting 34
"I Am Her Real Mother!" 35
Transracial Adoption 36
Searching 39
Gray Market, Black Market 41
The Most Important Thing 45
For More Information 46
Glossary/Index 46-48

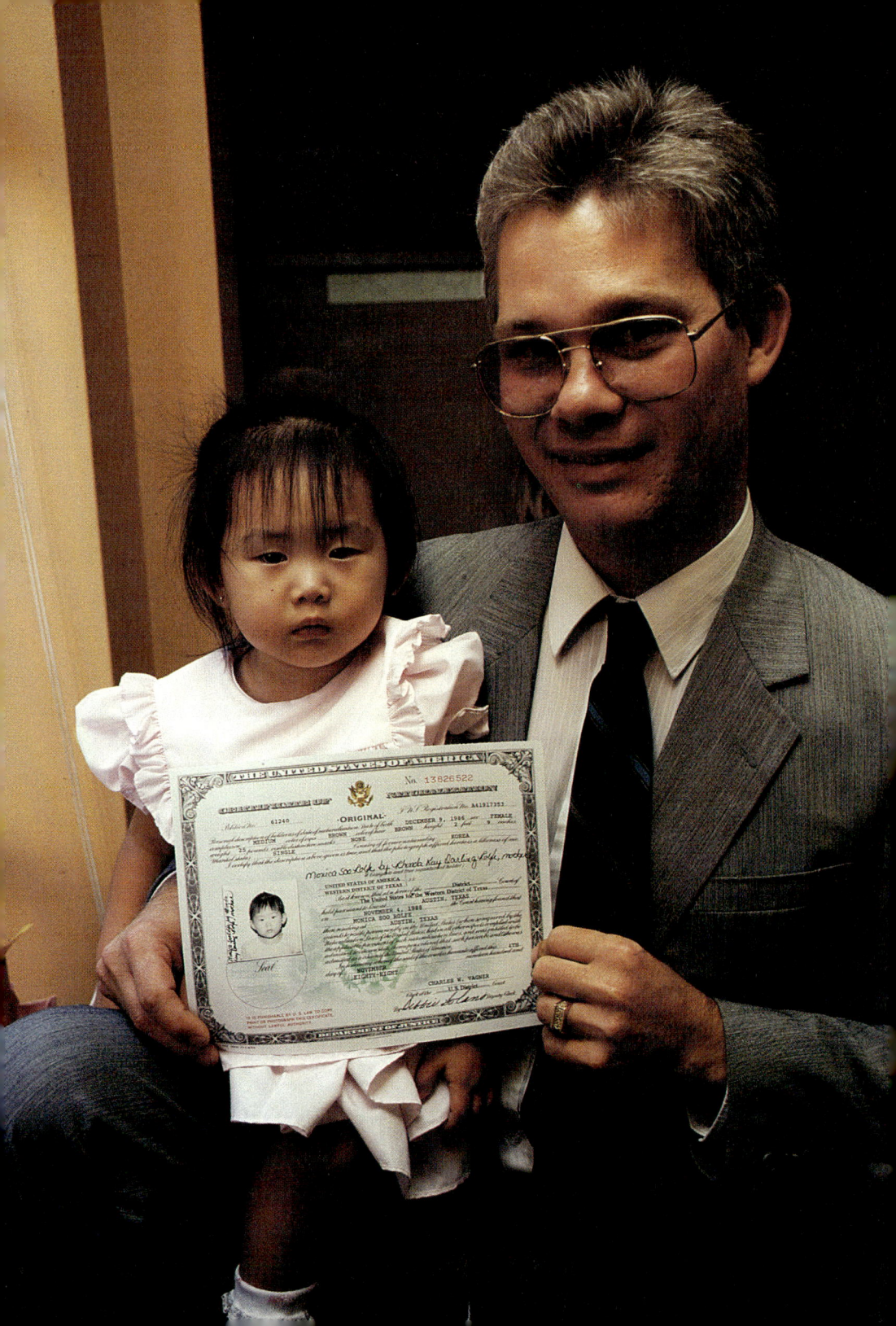

BEGINNINGS

When the voice over the airport loudspeaker announced another delay, the 76 people in the small waiting room groaned. Most of them had been sitting there for several hours already. Flight 58, on the last leg of its journey from Seoul, Korea, had been delayed more than 45 minutes at its stopover in Seattle. Now another hour would go by before it would land at Twin Cities International Airport in Minneapolis.

"I hope there's nothing wrong," murmured a woman who was holding a bunch of yellow balloons. "I hope the plane is all right."

An airline official nearby smiled sympathetically. "I'm sorry you have to wait so long. I've been told that the delay has nothing to do with a mechanical problem. I think it was just a foul-up with customs coming into the United States from Korea. Everything will be fine, I'm sure."

"Actually, we've been waiting for so many years, another hour shouldn't seem like much at all," said Tom Reynolds to his wife, Terry. She nodded, then stood, carefully putting down the large brown teddy bear she had been holding.

Terry said, "I can't just sit here any more. I'm going to walk over to the next concourse and back. I'll be back in a few minutes."

Tom nodded and leaned back in his chair. He looked around the waiting room and studied the people. Many

Adoptive parents must sometimes wait many years to adopt a child. But once that child arrives, the parents usually say the child was well worth the wait.

were talking in small groups, although none had met before this afternoon. There were 12 couples, most in their mid-30s. Most of them had some family with them —brothers or sisters, some parents as well.

Each of the couples seemed to understand why the waiting was difficult for the others. Each understood why so many grown-ups were standing around with bright signs, stuffed Mickey Mouses, and balloons.

All of these couples were waiting for children—their children. Yet, strangely, none of these people had ever seen their children before.

The children were coming to the United States for the first time, to people who wanted very much to *adopt* them into their own families. Each of the couples had waited, some for as long as two years, for the telephone call telling them their children were ready. Finally, on this chilly October afternoon, the children were on their way.

Most of the couples had requested healthy infants. One couple had sought a disabled child. A few, like Tom and Terry, had asked for older children. Their new daughter was almost two.

The Korean *adoption* agency had sent background information on each child to his or her adoptive parents. Tom and Terry knew, for example, the health history of their little girl. They knew that she had been quite small at birth, but that she had gained weight steadily. They knew something about the *birth mother* and *father* and the parents' health, too.

They had read a report from the woman who had been taking care of the child until her placement with an American family. The woman, known as a *foster parent,* told about the little girl's likes and dislikes, as well as her eating and sleeping habits. Armed with this information, Terry and Tom could help the little girl adjust more smoothly to life in their family.

The most precious data from the Korean agency, however, was a blurry photograph of the girl, taken about eight months before. It was getting worn around the edges because Tom and Terry had looked at it so often.

Finally the loudspeaker announced that the plane had arrived, and that the babies would be brought out after all the regular passengers had gotten off. The air in the waiting room felt electric. Now the couples stood quietly. New mothers and fathers pressed against the guard rails, watching the small door leading from the plane.

As the last regular travelers left the plane, several flight assistants hurried aboard. They were responsible for delivering each child to the right family.

The first assistant appeared at the entrance, holding a wailing bundle wrapped in a white blanket. The aide walked carefully over to a man and woman a few feet from Tom. She checked the names of the parents against her list, then carefully handed them the infant.

The next aide to appear held the hand of a very frightened boy of six or seven. As his new parents hugged the child, Terry saw the next aide walking toward them. She was carrying a little girl who was sound asleep. Tom had tears in his eyes, and Terry was biting her lower lip to keep from crying. Their little girl was here! "Hello," Terry whispered to the sleeping girl. "We've been waiting for you!"

The waiting room was coming alive again as the children were brought out. Forms were being signed. Babies were crying. Hugs and kisses were being exchanged.

The older children were more reserved. They seemed frightened by the noise and the confusion of the airport. Some stared soberly at the floor as their new parents tried to coax them into smiling at a camera.

Tom and Terry were proud to show their tiny daughter to her new grandparents. They posed for pictures and shook hands with some of the other new parents. Then it was time to put their daughter in her car seat and head home.

Many children in the world have no homes because one or both of their parents have died. A child may be separated from the mother because she is too sick or poor or for other reasons unable to care for him or her.

Adoption is a legal term for taking in someone else's child. Adoption is far more than a legal process, however. Adoptive parents agree to raise the child just as they would their *biological child*. They agree to be the mother and father of that child. Adoption gives a child a family; it gives a family a child to love and take care of.

Many children have no homes because one or both of their parents have died. Adoptive parents agree to raise these children as their own.

Adoption also gives adults and the children they adopt some special feelings and thoughts. What are these feelings? Why do people adopt? Why do some mothers and fathers let their children be adopted? What does it feel like to adopt somebody? What does it feel like to be adopted?

Adoption gives a child a family and gives a family a child to love and take care of.

ADOPTION – NOTHING NEW

Nobody knows when the first adoption took place. Historians do know that adoptions occurred in ancient cultures like Assyria, Egypt, Greece, and Rome.

One of the oldest bits of evidence is from the Code of Hammurabi. Hammurabi was a king of the Babylonian Empire, which was in southwestern Asia. He ruled for more than 40 years and was considered fair and wise.

10

The most famous of his accomplishments was the organizing and writing down of all the laws of his kingdom. The laws were engraved on an eight-foot-high stone. These laws—nearly 300 of them—were called the Code of Hammurabi. Many modern laws, including those concerning taxation, trade, and family matters, are based on this ancient code.

One of Hammurabi's laws dealt with the adoption process. The law stated that a child who was adopted could not be given back. The process was not reversible. Neither the adoptive parents nor the birth parents could change their minds. That law has survived from 1775 B.C. all the way to modern times!

APPRENTICES

In the early days of this country, *orphans*, or children whose parents had died, were common. Illnesses were dangerous. Antibiotics and shots that prevent disease had not yet been invented. Whole families, even whole villages, were wiped out by a single epidemic of flu or fever. Childbirth, too, was often dangerous. Historians estimate that 1 out of every 30 births resulted in the death of the mother.

When tragedies like these struck, the children were often taken in by a relative or a close neighbor. Even if a family didn't have much money, they would take in an orphaned relative. Besides, they often were glad to get an extra set of hands on the farm in exchange for providing food and shelter for the child!

Sometimes, however, an orphan had no friends or family. Then the child, particularly if it were a boy, was taken on as an *apprentice*. This meant that a craftsman in the town—blacksmith, carpenter, printer—would make an agreement with the child. He would be taught the master's craft and work for the master. In exchange, the master's family would raise him. When the boy was old enough, he would strike out on his own. The master got free labor, and the child got at least some sort of home.

Girls were usually not apprenticed, for in those days, they were expected only to grow up and to raise large families. Occasionally, though, homeless girls were taken in by families to help cook or baby-sit. And if she had a particularly kind family caring for her, a girl might be taught to sew or even read and write.

POORHOUSES: THE SHAME OF THE CITIES

The care of homeless children changed drastically in the nineteenth century. America was growing, and more and more people were arriving from all over the world. These people were called *immigrants*, and without even realizing it, they brought the end of the apprentice system.

With so many immigrants willing to work, craftsmen and other employers didn't have to use orphans. It was much easier to pay an adult a small wage for doing the work than to feed and clothe and train a young apprentice.

There were still plenty of children without families, however. Many wandered the streets, often becoming thieves and criminals at an early age. Others ended up in what were called *poorhouses*, or almshouses.

Poorhouses were large buildings found in almost every city. They were really dumping grounds for the people who had nowhere else to be. Elderly people who couldn't care for themselves, those who were dying but couldn't afford to see a doctor, entire penniless families, the disturbed or insane—all were sheltered in poorhouses.

But some people began to take a long look at poorhouse conditions. They were convinced that the death and noise and crowded conditions in them were not healthy for homeless children. Something needed to be done.

THE ORPHANAGE AND BEYOND

The *orphanage* was the answer these well-meaning people of the mid-nineteenth century found. An orphanage would usually house between 200 and 300 children, ranging from infants to teenagers.

The whole idea behind the orphanage was to provide a safe environment for children so they could grow into good citizens. If they were to remain around the poor, the ill, and the insane at the poorhouse, how could they learn discipline? How could they grow into respectable adults?

The children who lived in orphanages, therefore, were trained to be obedient. They were taught at an early age to march quietly from room to room. They were taught not to talk with other children, especially at mealtimes.

Unfortunately, those who ran the orphanages were not always kind to children who broke the rules. A child who was disrespectful was whipped or beaten, or put on a diet of bread and water, or confined to a cell.

Eventually, these orphanages came under attack. Some said that they were really no better than poorhouses; others said they were prisons. How could children be raised in such harsh conditions? They might be obedient, but they would be very unhappy.

Children seemed to flourish when they were raised in a family, when they had people to care about them. Perhaps, some of the critics argued, society should spend more time and effort in finding families who would raise these children.

Gradually, our country's adoption laws were written with these ideas in mind. The first state law making it possible for parents to raise someone else's children was

Today, children who are adopted have the same rights and privileges as any other children.

created in 1851. Now all 50 states have adoption laws. The laws state that adopted children have the same privileges and the same responsibilities as any other children. Things have certainly changed from the time of poorhouses a century before!

WHO ADOPTS?

There are many reasons children get separated from their biological parents, and an equal number of reasons why people choose to adopt a child. For some, the choice is purely voluntary. They choose not to bring a child into the world. They feel that giving birth to another person would only add to the overpopulation, pollution, or crime that already exists in the world. Many people who feel this way still want to raise children, so they adopt a child that has already been born.

Some people have medical conditions they fear their children could be born with. They choose adoption to prevent this from happening. With these people, too, the choice is voluntary—they could have children, but decide not to.

For many people, however, childlessness is not a matter of choice. They may have tried for years to have

Families have many different reasons for wanting to adopt a child.

children with no success. When this happens, they may seek help from their doctors. Sometimes the problem can be corrected, either through surgery or medication. But for a great number of couples, the condition cannot be corrected. When a person cannot have biological children of his or her own, it is called *infertility.*

When a couple finds out that they are infertile, they are often sad and angry. "It was the most painful part of our lives," said Dianne, a women in her early 30s. "All along we had planned on having two children. I was going to work until I was 27, then I would get pregnant. My husband and I felt cheated, as if we had been robbed of our dreams.

"It seemed for a while that the whole world was having babies. I couldn't turn on a TV show without seeing commercials for diapers or baby shampoos. Every woman I met on the street was pushing a baby stroller. I couldn't forget for a single minute that I would never know the feeling of being pregnant. It took my husband and me quite a while to realize that there is life beyond diapers."

DECIDING TO ADOPT

Some couples who cannot have their own biological children focus their lives in a different direction. For instance, they may decide to pursue their jobs or special interests. There are other couples, however, for whom the need to have children is strong. Even though they will never have a biological child, they want very much to have a child of their own, to become a family.

Mike and Robin are in their early 30s. They have been married for eight years. For the last three they've tried to have a baby. Last month, Robin's doctor told her that she was infertile. Both Mike and Robin were sad, but they are still sure they would like to be parents. Robin called an adoption agency 30 miles from their home and made an appointment to talk to someone. She and Mike are excited, but they have lots of questions.

At the agency they are met by a *social worker*. Her job is to answer questions, as well as to find out as much as possible about each couple who wishes to adopt. She listened carefully as Robin and Mike told about their trying to have a baby, and the doctor's findings. She nodded when they explained how much they wanted a family and that they were anxious to adopt a child.

"How does adoption work?" asked Mike. "What do we need to do to begin?"

The social worker explained that, in a way, the process had already begun when Robin and Mike decided they wanted to become adoptive parents. The process of adopting a child could be slow and frustrating at times, she said. The problem with adopting babies is that there are so few available.

WHERE ARE THE BABIES?

The social worker explained that things had changed drastically in the last 20 years. Back then there were far more babies than parents able to adopt them. Families did not have to wait at all. Often it was the babies who did the waiting.

Where have all the babies gone?

One reason the number of babies has declined is the access to *abortion*. In the past, most of the babies put up for adoption were born to unmarried teenagers. Abortion has been used for hundreds of years to end pregnancies. But it wasn't until 1973 that it was legalized in the United States. So many pregnant teenagers—as many as 40 percent—now choose to have abortions in clean, sanitary conditions rather than give birth.

Another reason that there are fewer available babies is that teenagers have learned how to prevent unwanted pregnancies with contraception. Birth control pills, condoms, and other forms of contraception are more available to teenagers and unmarried couples than they were before.

But probably the major reason for the shortage of babies, the social worker told Mike and Robin, has nothing to do with birth control or abortion. Rather, it is a difference in the way our society of today looks at unmarried mothers.

Years ago, a girl who was pregnant was a source of

shame and embarrassment to her family. Often, a pregnant teenager would hide her condition as long as she possibly could. Then, in the final few months of her pregnancy, she would mysteriously "disappear." Her family would spread the word that she had "gone away to visit relatives" or had "decided to spend some time traveling." The girl would go to a special home for unmarried mothers, usually run by a church. After her baby was born and handed over to an adoption agency, she would return home.

Now society no longer passes such harsh judgment on unmarried mothers. Some high schools even have facilities for day care for the babies. This helps young

Twenty years ago there were more babies available than adoptive parents. Today, however, adoptive parents must sometimes wait many years for a baby to become available.

mothers stay in school, so they can get better jobs to support their babies later on.

Since negative labels aren't applied to pregnant teenagers, many are now keeping their babies. Hundreds of thousands of babies that in the past would have been adoptable are now kept by their teenage mothers. In fact, by one estimate, 95 percent of all unmarried teenage mothers keep their babies.

For many of these girls, the thought of having a baby to dress and cuddle is almost irresistible. Having a little person who loves and needs them is naturally appealing.

But raising a baby is hard work. As the baby gets older and the mother grows up more herself, she may realize how difficult and time-consuming keeping the child is. Mothers who originally rejected the idea of adoption may be more interested as the child approaches 18 months or two or three years of age.

ON THE LIST

The social worker explained to Mike and Robin that this was why there were few infants ready to be adopted, but there were more older children.

Robin and Mike had strong feelings about their first child. They told the social worker that for a second or third child they might seek a toddler or even a child with a special problem. But their first had to be an infant. What should they do?

The social worker explained that they could be put on a waiting list for an infant. But before that happened they would have to be screened, or evaluated. The first step was filling out a long application form.

The form asked some easy-to-answer questions, such as "How many brothers and sisters did you have?" and "What kind of jobs do you have?" But there were also many questions that needed longer, more thoughtful answers. One question was about the kind of discipline they would use with a child in their family. Another asked them what their own parents' positive and negative points were.

A few weeks later they heard from the adoption agency again. Their application had been approved by the agency; the next step was a *home study*. The home study, as the social worker explained, is actually a series of three or four interviews conducted by an agency worker. The point is for him or her to talk with them, both individually and together, on a wide range of subjects. At least two of these interviews take place in the couple's home. This gives the agency a chance to see what kind of home the child would be placed in.

Mike and Robin were both nervous about the home study interviews. Would their house look too small to the agency workers? Should they have reupholstered that living room chair? The social worker told them their fears were common but unnecessary. The agency was not looking for couples with the most money or the biggest homes. What was important was that the home be a comfortable place for a child to live.

The questions in the interview were challenging. The interviewer asked Robin how she and Mike handled their disagreements. Mike was asked about his feelings on religion. Both Mike and Robin were exhausted after the social worker left.

The good news came several weeks later. Their interviewer felt they would make fine parents, the social worker told them. They were now officially on the list of couples waiting to adopt an infant. The agency worker couldn't tell them how long it would be until a baby would be available. Perhaps two years. Perhaps three or four. Mike and Robin's job now was simply to wait.

THE BIRTH MOTHER

When Connie was 15 years old, she found that she was pregnant. Her boyfriend was furious with her. How could she have let it happen? He didn't want anything to do with a baby. Connie knew she couldn't raise a baby alone, and she was far too young to be married even if her boyfriend had suggested it. What could she do?

Connie told her parents, probably the hardest thing she ever had to do. They were angry at first, as well as sad for Connie. But they would stick by her and try to help. One of the first things they did was make an

An adoption counselor talks with a pregnant young woman and her parents.

appointment to see a family counselor. There were several listed in the newspaper; the ads invited pregnant girls to come in and talk before deciding what to do.

The counselor was patient and helpful. She explained that Connie had several options—the first being abortion. Connie didn't have to have this baby.

An abortion sounded easy. She would miss a day of school, but after that, no one needed to know about what had happened. But Connie wasn't comfortable at all with abortion. That choice was fine for some other girls, she thought, but it wouldn't be right for her.

Connie was determined to give birth. Since adoption seemed to Connie to be the best idea, Connie's counselor gave her the name of another counselor at a nearby adoption agency.

DON'T DECIDE NOW

Connie and her parents had heard about healthy babies being in short supply at adoption agencies. Because of that, they expected the counselor to be more excited about Connie's decision. Connie expected to be asked to sign an agreement that very first day.

That didn't happen. In fact, the counselor at the agency was calm about Connie's decision. "We will help you in any way we can. If you plan to let us find good parents to raise this baby, we will need to know some information about you."

Connie spent some time answering questions about her health. Did she use drugs? Had she used alcohol during her pregnancy? Both of these could have an effect on the baby's health. What about her family's history of illness? What did she know about the health of the baby's father?

Questions like these are not meant to pry or cause embarrassment, the counselor explained. Rather, they help adoptive parents be on the lookout for illnesses that the baby might have inherited. For example, a child whose parents or grandparents had diabetes might have an increased risk of getting that disease.

As for signing any legal adoption papers that day, the counselor shook her head. "The last thing we want to do is to pressure you into any decision. Wait until your baby is born. Hold her, look at her. When you are certain, you can decide. This must be a decision you feel strong and good about."

A GIFT OF LIFE

Connie did eventually decide to put her baby, a girl, up for adoption. She was able to hold her baby and get to know her for a little while in the hospital. After she left the hospital, the agency counselor visited her.

"Sometimes I feel bad for what I'm doing," confessed Connie. "I know I'll never change my mind and decide to keep her. But I ask myself, 'What's wrong with me? How could someone abandon her own baby?'"

The counselor reassured Connie. "You're not abandoning her. You want what's best for her. You chose to give birth to her when you didn't have to go through with it. And now you are giving her a life of love. She'll have a mother and father who will love her and take care of her. You should never allow yourself to be ashamed of your decision."

The adoption of Connie's baby went by agency guidelines, which stated that Connie would not be told

Once a family is approved for an adoption, they are put on a waiting list. After a while, their adopted child finally arrives.

the names or address of the adoptive parents. Nor would her identity be known by the new parents.

There are a number of reasons for this rule. For one thing, the adoptive parents might worry that if the birth mother knew who they were and where they lived, she could try to make contact with the child. That could prove confusing and disruptive to their lives. At the same time, the birth mother also has a right to privacy. A child born to her when she was unmarried might be a part of her life she would like to keep to herself.

HOW DOES IT FEEL?

Most adoption agencies refer to *triads* in the adoption process. A triad refers to three sides in an adoption: the birth mother (and the birth father, if he is involved in the decision), the adoptive parents, and the child. If the adoption process is to be successful, the needs and feelings of each side must be thoughtfully considered.

We have talked about what the process is like for the birth mother and the adoptive parents. We have talked about the kinds of feelings many adoptive couples and birth mothers experience. But what about the children who are adopted? How do they feel about being adopted?

"I hardly ever think about it," said Sean, a tall, freckled boy of 12. "I was a baby when my mom and dad got me, so I don't remember my other mother at all. When my dad first explained it to me, I was about five. But I did worry when I was little about getting separated from my parents. I thought that since I got separated from my other mother, it could happen again, couldn't it? And what if I was bad? Maybe if I was really naughty, like if I didn't eat my supper, or if I talked back to my mom or dad, they might take me back to the adoption agency. I don't worry about that stuff anymore, though."

Many adopted children have experienced the same feelings as Sean. They know their parents love them.

They know there is a piece of paper somewhere that says that legally they are in the family forever. But still, they wonder. How come their other mothers let them go in the first place? Were they too naughty? Did they cry too much? And if they were disobedient at age six or seven or eight—would their adoptive parents let them go, too?

"My mom and dad used to tell me this story about how they went to this place—kind of like a hospital nursery. There were about 100 babies in these little cribs all in a line. My dad said they looked at all the babies there and chose me. I was their 'chosen girl' and I was special because of that," said 15-year-old Lisa.

But when Lisa was about seven, she worried about that story. "I sort of knew it couldn't really be true," she remembers. "I was worried, though. If I was such a great baby—if I was 'chosen' like my dad said, why did my first mother leave me? And there was something else that bothered me—the part about being chosen. Did my new parents expect me to be better than all those other kids? I don't think I'm that great. I don't want to be so different. I like being myself. But I used to worry if that would be good enough."

It seems as though the "chosen baby" story must have been a popular one for many years, judging by all the adopted children who have heard it! While some of those children enjoyed the story, others reacted as Lisa did. In fairness to the parents who used the "chosen baby" story to explain the adoption, it must be said that the parents had the best intentions. They didn't want their children to feel as though they had been given away or abandoned. The story was to make them feel special. Isn't it funny how a made-up story can backfire like that? Parents sometimes forget that being different in either a good or bad way is often difficult for children.

WONDERING

Patty is a dark-haired girl who just turned 13. She was adopted when she was two weeks old. Ever since she could remember, she has liked music. "It's funny because neither my mom nor dad are musical," she said. "I can pick up an instrument and pretty much figure it out. I'm not a genius or anything, but I have a talent for music."

Patty sometimes wonders if either of her birth parents was musical. "Everybody knows that our environment is important. Who you are lots of times is shaped by how you are treated, what kinds of experiences you have as you are growing up. But some of who I am might be tied into two other people who I've never met. That's an odd feeling. Maybe my mother—my birth mother, I mean—is a composer or a concert pianist." She giggled. "Maybe she and my birth father were famous rock stars!"

Most adopted children go through a time in their

lives when they think a lot about their birth parents. It may start right away when their adoptive parents first explain the situation. A child of four or five, however, is not really interested in or capable of understanding a detailed explanation. Just hearing that "a big airplane brought me to Mommy and Daddy" or "I grew in another lady's tummy, but my mommy and daddy brought me home" is enough to satisfy the curiosity of a young child.

As the child gets older, however, his or her questions may be more specific. Sometimes the child doesn't even ask the questions he is feeling. "Late at night," says Evan, "I lie in bed and pretend that my other parents

Many adopted children wonder about their birth parents. As they get older, they may have more questions and want more specific answers about their birth parents.

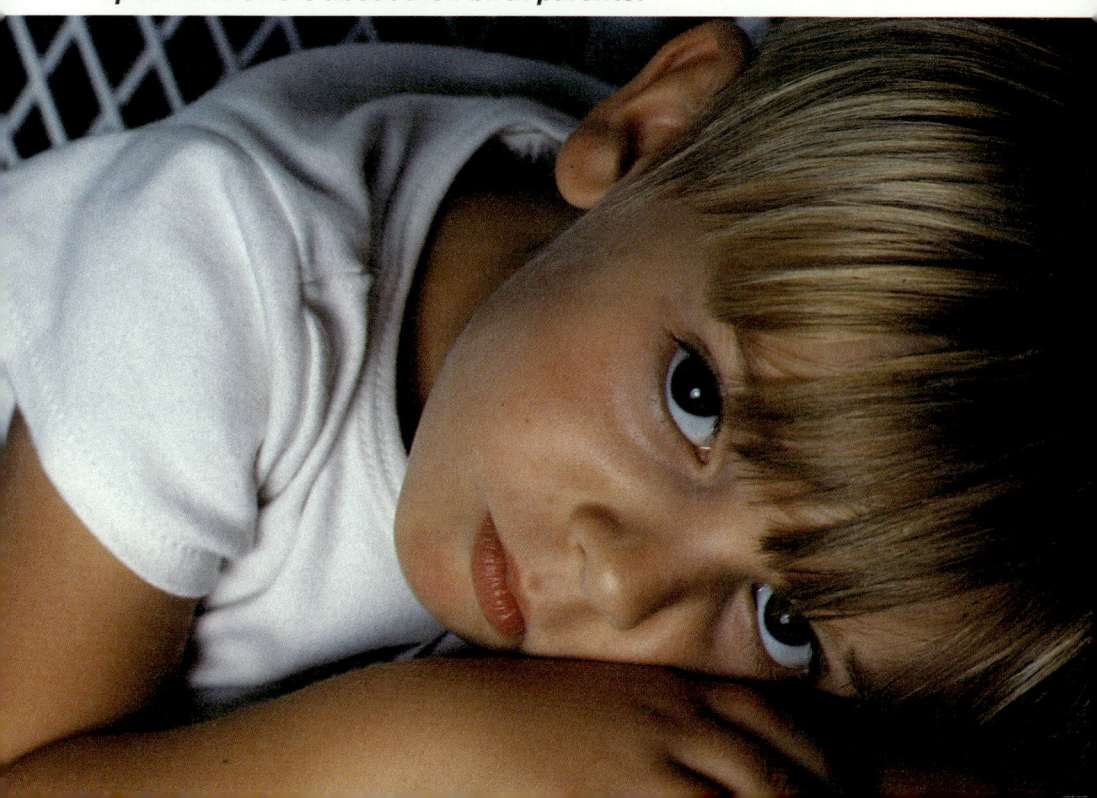

Usually, the adoptive parents will tell their child all they know about the child's birth parents.

are famous. I think about how I could tell everybody in my school that I am the son of a sports star or a hero. Sometimes when I'm mad at my mom and dad I think to myself that my birth parents wouldn't be so mean to me. They'd let me go camping every weekend. They'd give me seconds on dessert."

Christine agrees. She is nine, but she remembers that when she was little she used to pretend that her birth mother was a beautiful princess. "I thought that she would meet me someday and say, 'Boy, you sure are pretty. You look just like me!'"

It's normal for adopted children to wonder about these things. Often they deal with anger and hurt feelings by saying, "Of course, my birth mother would be more understanding." And who wouldn't be intrigued by the idea of someone out there who maybe looks a little like them?

An adopted child usually gets help from parents who try to answer his or her questions as truthfully as possible. By sharing some information — no matter how sketchy — about the birth mother, the parents are showing the child that it is all right to have questions and to wonder. For instance, the parents could say, "We don't know much about her, but she must have loved you very much to go through with a pregnancy when she was not married." As one agency counselor says, "It's simply a matter of keeping the lines of communication open both ways."

Yet some parents are a little frightened when their adopted child questions them about the birth parents. "I felt like it was a knife going through me at first," admitted one adoptive mother. "Every time Jake asked about his birth mother, I felt threatened. Why was he asking? Didn't he love me? Would he rather have her as a mother? It took me a while to put everything in perspective. Jake was asking only because he wanted to know. He needed reassurance from me that it was okay to wonder."

WORDS CAN STING

Some of life's most painful moments can be caused by words—or the cruel use of them. The old playground chant "Sticks and stones can break my bones, but names will never hurt me" is nonsense. Anyone who has ever been taunted with names like "dummy" or "fatty" can tell you so.

Adopted children sometimes face cruel or thoughtless use of words. The term *adopted* can be used in a very negative way.

"I used to hate it when some of the kids would say, 'That kid's adopted. Nobody wanted him,'" said Billy, now a high school senior. "I knew it was only a dumb thing for them to say. I knew it wasn't even a little bit true. But it still made me feel bad."

The word *illegitimate* is another term that has caused pain to adopted children and their families. Illegitimate means "not legal," and it has to do with whether or not a child can legally claim the father's inheritance. Long ago, children who were born "out of wedlock"—in other words, to unmarried parents—were called illegitimate and were prevented from inheriting money or property.

That isn't the case today. Adopted children who are born to unmarried parents have the same rights as any other children. Some people still use the word *illegitimate,* however, to refer to adopted children. The word can hurt, because it makes the child feel as though he or she isn't quite legal, or isn't quite as good as a child born to married parents.

"I AM HER REAL MOTHER!"

Adopted children are not the only ones who can be hurt by the misuse of words. Many adoptive parents, too, have been stung, especially by the word *real*.

Parents of adopted children do all the same things other parents do. They work hard to make a good home for their children. They may attend PTA meetings, be Girl Scout leaders, and go to school concerts. They stay up all night with their children when they've got the flu. They read to their children and take them to baseball games.

It's no wonder, then, that adoptive parents flinch when someone refers to their child's birth mother and father as the "real parents."

Margaret Jensen has two children—both adopted. "I resent it when people refer to the birth mother of an adopted child as being her 'real mother.' I am the only mother my daughters can remember. They came from India when they were only a few months old. My husband and I clothe them and feed them and love them enormously. We took out the loan for braces for their teeth. We taught them how to ride a bicycle, and we discipline them when they misbehave. I stayed up half the night sewing their Halloween costumes. So when my neighbor said, 'Why, Margaret, you are as busy as a real mother,' I wanted to slug her!"

Adopted children know the difference, though. Most are aware that they had a mother who gave birth to them, but that she could not be their mother. As eight-year-old Steven explains, "I grew in my birth mom's tummy. She did a good thing in letting me be born so I could go live with my real mom and dad. One time I got mad at my dad and said that he was mean to me. I said that my real dad would never be so mean. But he said, 'Steven, I am your real dad.' I knew he was right."

TRANSRACIAL ADOPTION

For a variety of reasons, most couples seeking to adopt children are white, while many of the available babies are black or foreign-born. This has led to controversy. *Transracial adoption* is the adoption of a child by parents of a different race. In the last decade, transracial adoption has become more common, but there are differing opinions on whether it is a good thing.

Many people support transracial adoption. They say the children are better off in a family of a different race than no family at all.

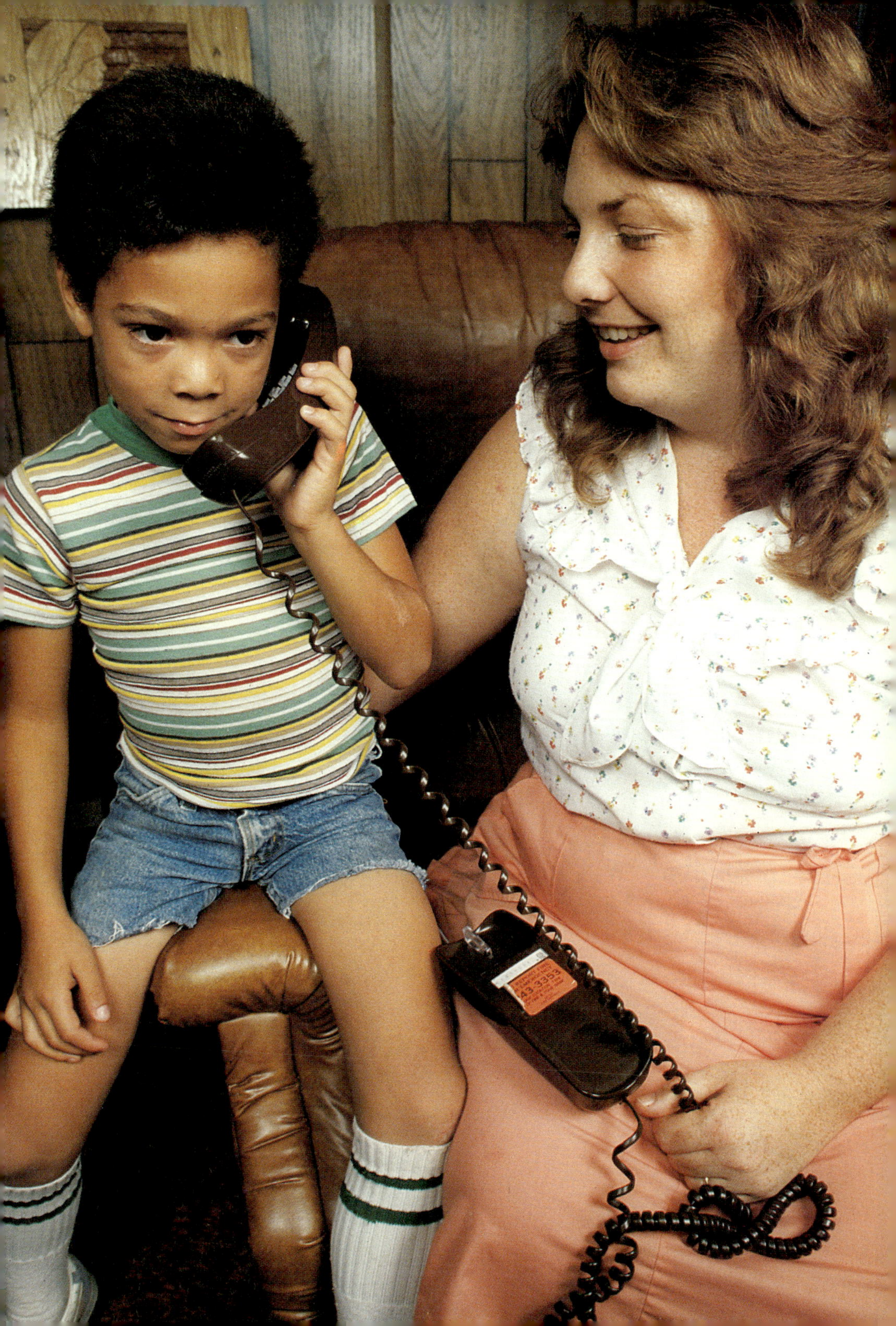

Some think that it is wrong for white parents to try to raise a child who is, for example, black or Asian. They point to the confusion the child will feel as he or she gets older. The little girl arriving from Korea mentioned at the beginning of this book, for instance, might wonder someday about her identity. She might think: Am I Korean or am I an American? Being raised in an environment that is predominantly white, it would be easy to forget her Korean heritage. Would it matter if she did?

Other problems can also come up in transracial families. A white family that has adopted a black child, for example, will probably hear negative racial comments. Relatives may also treat the black child differently than they would a white child. David and Cynthia adopted a black baby two years ago. "We told everyone we were getting our baby, and that he was black. Nobody seemed to react badly to the news. But when we named him Paul, my grandparents hit the roof. Paul was the name of my uncle, and they thought it was outrageous to give the name to a black child."

However, there are many who support the notion of transracial adoption. They say that since there are so many white families who want babies and so many black and foreign-born babies waiting to be adopted, why make a big issue out of it? The point, they say, is that children are better off in a family of a different race than with no family at all. The obstacles can be overcome, say supporters.

Indeed, many agencies that place black and foreign-born children in white families offer support services to these families. They urge the parents to take an active role in explaining to the child that he or she has a double heritage. Learning as much as possible about the country of their birth or about the black experience can help adopted children and their families. It can be challenging, say supporters of transracial adoption, but the rewards far outweigh the problems.

SEARCHING

There is an aspect of adoption that often causes nervousness and fear in adoptive parents. That is the curiosity children feel about their birth parents. Children often satisfy this by talking to their adoptive parents. Parents can explain what they know about the child's birth mother or father from what they were told at the agency.

But some children are not willing to go through their whole lives wondering. They want to know more than their parents can tell them. They need to get answers to their questions. Who were my birth parents? Why couldn't they keep me? Do I look like somebody else? Do I have biological brothers or sisters somewhere?

Some adopted children decide to search for their birth parents. It's not, they say, because they don't love their real parents. "I wouldn't do anything to hurt

Mom and Dad," says Sally. "But I'm 14 and I really want to know my own roots. I thought my parents would want to talk about it, but they acted like I was betraying them or something."

Searching for birth parents is like putting together a jigsaw puzzle when you don't know whether you have all the pieces. In most states, the adopted child's records are sealed, which means that he or she is not permitted to read them. The purpose behind this secrecy has always been to protect the child. It was important to make sure that birth parents didn't change their minds years after the child had been adopted and try to take him or her back.

The agency can answer some questions. For instance, they may be able to tell the child the occupation of the mother and her nationality, but not her name or address. Even so, some adopted children can find out enough information from old newspapers or hospital files to stay on the trail of a birth parent. In some cases, they are successful.

Statistically, only about two percent of adopted children ever conduct such a search. For some of those who do, the experience is exciting. They are thrilled to talk to a blood relative and get answers to questions they'd had for years. But for others the search ends in disappointment. The birth mother may be angry that she's been found. She might have a family that she has never told about this child. How could she explain the appearance of a child from her past no one knows about?

There are many opposing views on the searching process. Some say the files should not be sealed. If someone wants to know his or her family history, they say, it's their own business. Certainly an agency can't withhold information like that.

But there are others who insist that opening the files could cause embarrassment to the birth parents, as well as hurt feelings in the adoptive parents. Just how the controversy will be resolved is unclear. Will the law about sealed files and records be changed? This will be an issue we'll be hearing about in the coming years.

GRAY MARKET, BLACK MARKET

Another controversy that has gained attention on television and in newspapers lately is the high number of people adopting infants through *private adoptions*. In a private adoption, the couple doesn't find a child through an agency at all. Instead, they find a birth mother on their own. They may take out an ad in the newspaper or ask doctors to look for a young woman who is planning not to keep her baby. A lawyer usually acts as the go-between in the dealings between the birth mother and the adoptive couple.

Many young mothers feel bad about "simply handing over" their newborn baby to an agency. They would like some reassurance that the baby will be adopted by good parents. A private adoption can give them the peace of mind they need.

Many adoptive parents, too, prefer to go the private route. They may have felt that an agency had standards they couldn't meet. Perhaps they were older than the agency guidelines allowed. They may have felt the interviews were an invasion of their privacy. The best aspect of a private adoption, however, is usually the shorter wait.

"My husband was 42 when we adopted our baby," said Barbara. "No agency lets you adopt an infant if you are more than 38 or 39. We asked around at some clinics. One afternoon a nurse called me and said that there had been a young girl talking about giving up her baby. The girl wanted to meet us—that was her idea—but we could have the baby immediately after it was born.

"Our wait was less than three months. No agency would have helped us that soon even if we had met the age requirement."

Critics of private adoption, however, say that it can fail in a number of ways. Unlike an adoption agency that carefully screens all couples, the private adoption simply offers a legal contract. No one evaluates the couple beforehand. The birth mother who wishes to meet the adoptive parents may get a quick first impression, but that is all.

Another failing of the private adoption method, some say, is that the couples who get the babies are often the ones with the most expensive lawyers or the most connections. In some private adoptions, couples agree to pay all or most of the birth mother's medical expenses, in addition to the lawyer's fees. Because of the emphasis on money, and because there are no set fees as there are with an adoption agency, private adoption is often called the "gray market."

The term *gray market* is to distinguish this type of adoption from another, highly illegal, method, called

Some parents do not want to wait years to adopt a child. They might go through a private agency to find their baby.

black market adoption. Black market adoption is the actual buying and selling of newborn babies to wealthy childless couples. In a black market operation, a go-between—usually a lawyer—will seek out pregnant women who plan to give up their babies.

"Usually, the lawyer will promise the girl that he can get her hospital expenses paid for," reports an undercover policeman who has made arrests of such lawyers. "He tells the girl that if she keeps her mouth shut about the deal, there will be an extra $5,000 for her trouble. Then he goes to the couple and tells them that he can get them a healthy white infant, but it will cost them quite a bit.

"Unfortunately, the couple is usually so desperate to have a child that they don't mind paying the money. I've heard of babies being sold for $75,000! The lawyer makes a huge profit, you can be sure of that."

It's important to note that a private adoption isn't the same as a black market baby operation. Often private adoptions work out just fine. They are called gray market, however, because they might lead to trouble. If one of the parties involved—say a lawyer, or a doctor, or even the birth mother herself—wants to make a profit, the opportunity is there. A good private adoption depends upon the honesty of the participants.

THE MOST IMPORTANT THING

You may well continue to read about adoption in the newspaper or hear about it on radio and TV in the coming months. Questions about the rights of the birth parents, the adoptive parents, and especially the adopted child are capturing headlines. Should adopted children have the right to read their confidential files? Should private adoptions be regulated by the state? Should single people be allowed to adopt babies? What will become of the teenage mothers who keep their babies for a year or two before giving them up for adoption? What will become of the babies themselves?

These questions arise naturally when people are concerned about adoption. Yet the most important question of all is the one posed by the judge the day the adoptive parents and their new child go to court to make the adoption legal: "Do you promise to love this child, to take him into your family and make a home for him?"

The most important part of adoption is that babies or young children can grow up with a loving family.

FOR MORE INFORMATION

For more information about adoption, write to:

North American Center on Adoption
67 Irving Place
New York, NY 10003

GLOSSARY/INDEX

ABORTION 19, 24—*Ending a pregnancy in the early months by removing the fetus from the uterus.*
ADOPTION 6, 8, 9, 10, 11, 14, 15, 16, 17, 18, 19, 20, 21, 22, 23, 25, 26, 28, 29, 30, 34, 36, 38, 39, 40, 41, 42, 43, 44, 45—*The legal raising of a child by a family other than his or her birth parents.*
APPRENTICE 11, 12—*A young child, usually a boy, who is taken in by a master craftsman and his family. The apprentice helps his master free of charge; in exchange, the master teaches the child a trade and provides him with food and shelter.*
BIOLOGICAL CHILD 8, 17, 18—*A child born to parents, not adopted.*
BIRTH FATHER 6, 28, 35, 39—*The man who is an adopted child's biological father.*
BIRTH MOTHER 6, 27, 28, 30, 33, 35, 36, 39, 40, 42, 45—*The woman who is an adopted child's biological mother; the woman who gave birth to the child.*

GLOSSARY/INDEX

BLACK MARKET ADOPTION 41, 44—*The illegal selling of infants to adoptive couples.*

FOSTER PARENTS 7—*Those who care for a child during the waiting period before he or she is placed in the adoptive parents' home.*

GRAY MARKET 41, 43, 45—*Another term for private adoption, so called because it carries the possibilities of babies being "sold."*

HOME STUDY 22—*A series of interviews a couple must take part in if they want to adopt a child through an adoption agency. The purpose of the interviews is to determine whether or not the people will make good parents.*

ILLEGITIMATE 34, 35—*A term meaning "not legal." It used to refer to a child whose birth parents were not married.*

IMMIGRANT 12, 13—*One who moves from the country he or she was born in to live in another.*

INFERTILITY 17, 18—*A medical condition that makes it impossible for a man to impregnate a woman, or for a woman to become pregnant.*

ORPHAN 11, 12, 13—*A child whose parents have died.*

ORPHANAGE 13, 14—*An institution for children who do not have parents.*

POORHOUSE 12, 13—*Existed in the early years of this country. A poorhouse was a shelter for orphans,*

GLOSSARY/INDEX

poor or homeless people, the elderly, and the insane.
PRIVATE ADOPTION 41, 42, 43, 44, 45—*The process of adopting a child without going through an adoption agency. Private adoptions are usually handled by a lawyer or another go-between for the birth mother and adoptive couple.*
REAL PARENTS 35, 36—*Those who raise a child and love and care for her or him.*
SOCIAL WORKER 18, 19, 21, 22, 23—*A person who helps other people solve problems with their family, their jobs, or other areas. One of a social worker's jobs is to work with people who want to adopt a child.*
TRANSRACIAL ADOPTION 36, 38, 39—*Adoption of a child of one race by parents of another. The most common in this country in this decade is the adoption of black (African-American) or foreign-born Asian children by white couples.*
TRIAD 28—*The three groups involved in the adoption process. The triad includes the birth mother, the adoptive parents, and the child.*